P9-EGN-189

NELL HILL'S
Entertaining in Style

Cider

NELL HILL'S
Entertaining in Style

INSPIRING PARTIES AND
SEASONAL CELEBRATIONS

MARY CAROL GARRITY

WITH JEAN LOWE AND MICKI CHESTNUT

PHOTOGRAPHY BY BRYAN E. McCAY

**Andrews McMeel
Publishing, LLC**
Kansas City

STYLIST
Kerri Wagner

CONTRIBUTING EDITORS

Marsee Bates	Barbara Fricke
Gloria Case	Brenda Graves
Lynda Coulter	Dianne Howard

Ann Humphreys

❧

NELL HILL'S
Entertaining in Style

❧

Copyright © 2006 by Nell Hill's, Inc.
Photography copyright © by Bryan E. McCay.

All rights reserved. Printed in China. No part of this book may be used or reproduced in any manner whatsoever without written permission except in the case of reprints in the context of reviews. For information write Andrews McMeel Publishing, LLC, an Andrews McMeel Universal company, 4520 Main Street, Kansas City, Missouri 64111.

06 07 08 09 10 WKT 10 9 8 7 6 5 4 3 2 1

Garrity, Mary Carol.
   Nell Hill's entertaining in style: inspiring parties and seasonal celebrations/Mary Carol Garrity, with Jean Lowe and Micki Chestnut: photography by Bryan E. McCay.
    p. cm.
   ISBN-13: 978-0-7407-6052-5
   ISBN-10: 0-7407-6052-1
    1. Entertaining. 2. Parties. 3.Party decorations.
    I. Lowe, Jean. II. Chestnut, Micki. III. Title.

TX731.G265 2006
793.2—dc22

                         2006042769

Book design by Diane Marsh

ATTENTION: SCHOOLS AND BUSINESSES
Andrews McMeel books are available at quantity discounts with bulk purchase for educational, business, or sales promotional use. For information, please write to: Special Sales Department, Andrews McMeel Publishing, LLC, 4520 Main Street, Kansas City, Missouri 64111.

To my stylish mother, Mary Lou Diebolt,
who still delivers my lunch every day
to Nell Hill's. The little brown lunch bag
with the peanut butter and jelly sandwich
is the highlight of my day.

Contents

Introduction

※

I ABSOLUTELY LOVE TO ENTERTAIN. NOTHING GETS MY CREATIVE JUICES FLOWING MORE THAN PLANNING AND HOSTING—OR ATTENDING—A PARTY, WHETHER IT BE A SWANK RECEPTION OR A CASUAL GET-TOGETHER WITH A FEW GOOD FRIENDS.

PERHAPS I INHERITED THIS GREAT LOVE OF CELEBRATION FROM MY GRANDMOTHER NELL HILL, FOR WHOM I NAMED MY FIRST HOME FURNISHINGS EMPORIUM. AN IRISH IMMIGRANT AND EARLY KANSAS PIONEER, NELL MADE EVERYONE WHO ENTERED HER HOME FEEL LIKE THE MOST SPECIAL PERSON ON EARTH. I STRIVE TO REFLECT THAT SAME SPIRIT EVERY TIME I OPEN MY DOORS TO VISITORS.

Entertaining comes as naturally

for me as it does for my hometown. Atchison, Kansas, has warmly greeted visitors for hundreds of years, starting with famed explorers Lewis and Clark, who picked this beautiful spot on the Missouri River to dock their boats and celebrate Independence Day. With the thriving Atchison, Topeka & Santa Fe Railroad, lumber and railroad barons made Atchison their home, building grand homes high on the river bluffs. One of these was the childhood home of Atchison's most famous daughter, the gutsy aviator Amelia Earhart.

My husband, Dan, and I jumped at the chance to renovate one of the town's fabulous historic homes, and over a decade, sank more time and money into our fixer-upper than we want to admit. Even before our 130-year-old Greek Revival was finished, I was already planning the parties I would throw there. Like my grandma Nell, I like to keep my home filled with the laughter of friends and family.

Through the years, many of my friends, family, and customers have confided that they too would love to entertain more often, but they are intimidated by planning and pulling off a party. Some are at a loss for how to decorate their homes for special events. Others become overwhelmed by the thought of creating a culinary feast. But most are just stalled and need a spark of inspiration to fuel their natural creativity.

The advice I share with them is always the same: Develop your own style of entertaining, because when you entertain in a manner that comes naturally to you, you'll have as much fun hosting the gathering as your guests will have attending it.

For instance, my favorite part of party planning is decorating to create a dazzling first impression. I like to go all out when building the kind of drama and mood my guests will long remember. My reliable tools include gorgeous seasonal accents, which I weave throughout my home's decor, and beautiful tableware like china, crystal, silver, and linens, which, when carefully combined, can really wow guests.

You'll see my love for entertaining reflected in my three home furnishings stores. We've filled gallery after gallery with treasures you can use to add spark to your

home's interior and exterior, plus loads of dining items essential for creating unusual and memorable tables for all your events. We're thrilled to work with visitors who travel here from across the region (and even from both coasts), helping them discover new ways to mix and match pieces to make their homes—and events—truly unique, entirely personal, and always remarkable.

It's this passion for inventive entertaining that prompted me to write *Nell Hill's Entertaining in Style*. I've been dying to pass on the creative ideas, secret tips, and practical techniques I've gleaned from years of throwing my own parties and attending events in the homes of others. In these pages, we'll introduce you to the Nell Hill's style of entertaining, brought to life through the parties and celebrations at my home and those of a few dear friends.

Through the twenty-five years I've been lucky enough to own Nell Hill's, my customers and friends have shared with me one-of-a-kind ideas for parties. These folks are marvels—they can put together a fabulous fete faster than I can restock the store. These are among the best parties I've ever attended, and in this book, we'll tell you how the hostesses pulled each one off with relative ease.

Since decorating is my passion, I've included my personal favorite ideas to help make your home simply stunning for every event you host. In the pages that follow, we'll share professional styling tips, like how-to's for creating an entry that makes an indelible first impression. You'll gain step-by-step instructions for building dining room displays so creative that we hope your guests will be speechless. And we'll pass on ways to incorporate the natural beauty and bounty of each season into every room of your house.

We'll also talk about how to create a menu for your celebration filled with food that's delicious and so simple to make and buy. I firmly believe party fare should be easy to prepare so you can spend your time enjoying friends, not slaving over the stove. Since I'm not a chef—okay, I'm actually a disaster in the kitchen—I often have my parties catered. Other times, I call on Dan or my friend Cheryl Hartell, owner of the Vineyards Restaurant, a trendy bistro in nearby Weston, Missouri, to come to my rescue in the kitchen.

Luckily, I have many friends for whom cooking is an art form. We'll visit their kitchens and see what savory dishes they make for their guests. And though this book is most definitely not a cookbook, we'll share a few yummy recipes you won't find anywhere else.

As you read through Nell Hill's *Entertaining in Style*, you'll see that all the events I've showcased concentrate on the fun, fanciful, and fantastic. I just know as you see the wonderful parties presented here, you'll be inspired, just as I was, to start planning your own event, whether a gathering of friends or your family's next holiday meal. So, please come in and enjoy. May this book be a muse that lights your imagination. Now, let's have fun!

Mary Carol Garrity

Fat Tuesday
Ladies' Luncheon
Easter Brunch
Dining Under the Stars

PART ONE

Spring

*The spirit of entertaining is reborn as we're inspired by
the season's wonderful color schemes, fresh air, and a host
of reasons to bring people together.*

❧

WHEN I LOOK OUT OUR KITCHEN WINDOW AND SEE THE FIRST ROBINS

OF THE SEASON HOPPING ABOUT IN MY COURTYARD, MY HEART LIFTS. SPRING

IS HERE! AFTER THE LONG, GRAY MIDWESTERN WINTER, THESE FEATHERED

HERALDS OF SPRINGTIME JOYFULLY ANNOUNCE THAT, SOON, THE EARTH WILL

COME ALIVE AGAIN.

As winter melts away,

I feel rejuvenated and am consumed by an irrepressible itch to welcome in this blissful season with my friends and family. After months of hibernation, I'm ready to frolic.

Before I pull out my calendar to plan the springtime's social revelries, I first set the stage for entertaining by lightening and brightening my home's interior to reflect the fresh, new season. I might repaint a drab room or re-cover a sofa that's a bit tattered and worn. But the most common way I open my arms to spring is to re-create the beauty of nature on display just outside my window.

In the early months of spring, my cats launch their seasonal battle with the birds. My husband, Dan, and I roll with laughter as we watch their antics—the feline fighters yowl with frustration as the lightning-fast birds swoop down from the trees and give them a peck on the head.

Like my cats, I can't resist birds. One of our approaches to decorating at Nell Hill's is to surround yourself with things you love. So every spring, I showcase these quirky creatures in my home decorating. Through the years, I've collected bird figurines in terra-cotta, iron, silver, and glass, and I perch this avian assortment in unexpected places all over my house.

Why not build drama through your home using your collectibles? Here are some of the ways I weave my bevy of birds into nearly every room of my home each spring.

It's simple to carry a bird theme throughout your house. Hang a glass lantern on your exterior door filled with faux cuttings from flowering spring shrubs, then tuck a bird's nest in the crook of one of the branches. You can even add a bird print as a backdrop, as I did on my front door this spring. Or give a bird's nest filled with blue eggs a place of honor in your living room, placing it on a silver cake plate under a cloche on the mantel.

When setting my dining room table for an early spring dinner party, I let the whole display go to the birds. For a centerpiece, I create three risers out of attractive bird-watching books. On top of the risers, I position candlesticks topped with birds' nests filled with speckled eggs. To add more layers and intrigue to this tableau, I put a small, weathered birdcage in the center of the display, then add a pair of antique field glasses. For a realistic touch, I sprinkle birdseed around the table.

To create interesting layers in your place settings, start with a twiggy place mat topped by dinnerware featuring birds. Then, land a bird figurine in the center of the salad plate. Tie each linen napkin with a piece of jute and tuck in a feather.

Another way I welcome spring into my home is by decorating with seasonal flowers. The first thing my guests see when they visit during this sublime season is a joyful bouquet of early blooms. Since I'm not lucky enough to have a host of spring-blooming bushes in my yard, I rely on artificials. Honestly, I can't tell the difference.

I like to fill a rustic garden urn with leggy forsythias or azalea branches, then give the arrangement center stage in my entryway. On the table next to my front door, I often feature a beautiful planter holding fragrant paperwhites or hyacinths.

To add a touch of seasonal color and romance to that hard-to-decorate space on top of my bookcases or armoire, I crown them with picking baskets filled with a hefty gathering of delicate pink crabapple boughs, letting the branches cascade willy-nilly over the front and side.

Or, if you want a display that's an absolute showstopper, suspend a bare tree branch from the ceiling in the dining room or living room. Then, entwine the foliage of spring-blooming shrubs or vines through the branches. Try it with vibrant forsythia blooms, and you'll feel like you're walking under a spray of sunlight. Or, hang dollops of purple wisteria clusters to create an inviting retreat. To add to the enchantment, suspend baubles from the branches, like prisms, paper lanterns, or glass votives.

Once my home shines with spring, I can't wait to fill it with guests. And I eagerly anticipate receiving invitations to my friends' seasonal celebrations.

Fat Tuesday

A MARDI GRAS PARTY TO REMEMBER

❦

One invitation I look forward to every year is the annual Mardi Gras gala hosted by my friends Ann and Guy Humphreys. This Fat Tuesday festival started out as an impromptu gathering of neighbors who were just looking for an excuse to celebrate spring's imminent arrival. In the ensuing years, the party has evolved into an elaborate event that packs as much fun as you can have this far from Bourbon Street.

I had no idea Ann and Guy threw this delightful party until I happened upon it by accident. I was taking a rare day off from Nell Hill's to shop with friends when an ice storm hit and made the roads impassable. I crept to the Humphreys' house and was thrilled to not only find safe shelter, but the chance to crash their Mardi Gras party.

Every year the preparty begins at dusk when Ann, Guy, and their friends gather together in her kitchen to create the evening's feast. When I first met Ann, we formed an instant bond as the only noncooks in a group of

Formal balls, parties in the streets, and parades with floats celebrate the

rich traditions of the New Orleans Mardi Gras.

Bring the same tradition to life with this colorful party plan

and celebrate in style with your friends.

❧

gourmets. Ann has overcome her kitchen phobia and now is a fabulous chef. I, however, am still culinary–challenged, but I happily plop myself down in the midst of the cooks, ready to lend a hand or sample the fare.

The interior of the Humphreys' 1950s sprawling brick ranch is a marvelous example of the Nell Hill's approach to decorating. They've created a comfortable retreat filled with things they love, artfully mixing timeless treasures with seasonal accents.

Ann follows this same approach when she decorates for events like her Mardi Gras party. Just steps from the front door, she's already set the scene for fun. Guests are greeted by a butler's table filled with everything they'll need to start celebrating—Mardi Gras masks, colored beads, and tall glasses of New Orleans vodka freezes, all beautifully displayed by candlelight.

Then, the decorations in the dining room really bring the party to life. Ann has collected a beautiful array of serving pieces and table accents that are put to good use at this signature event. Layer by layer, Ann creates a table display exploding with energy and excitement, yet infused with a touch of mystery and intrigue.

❧

EACH YEAR FOR THE LAST FIVE YEARS, ANN HAS COME UP WITH A CLEVER WAY TO SHOWCASE THE MENU. THIS YEAR'S OFFERING IS PRINTED ON VELLUM PAPER AND AFFIXED TO THE BACK OF MASKS. THE MASKS ARE MOUNTED ON GREEN DOWELS, THEN PLACED AT THE ENDS OF THE TABLE AND ON THE CENTERPIECE. MENUS FROM THE HUMPHREYS' PAST MARDI GRAS PARTIES ARE DISPLAYED ON A TRAY IN THE ENTRY TO THEIR HOME.

THE WARM GLOW OF THE CHANDELIER, AN ANTIQUE CENTERPIECE HOLDING DEEP RED TULIPS, AND THE SPARKLE OF COLORFUL BEADS MIX WITH A HOST OF OTHER CLEVER DETAILS TO SET THE SCENE FOR AN EVENING OF REVELRY, GOOD FOOD, AND FRIENDSHIP. WHAT STARTED OUT AS A LAST-MINUTE GATHERING OF FRIENDS AND NEIGHBORS ON A FROST-COVERED EVENING HAS TURNED INTO ONE OF EVERYONE'S FAVORITE EVENTS.

SIMPLE PLACE CARDS MADE WITH FOIL STICKERS TOP THE FLUTED COMPOTES THAT WILL HOLD SEAFOOD CAKE APPETIZERS. BLACK PLACE MATS OF WOVEN STRAW, ANCHOR THE PLACE SETTINGS OF CREAMY-WHITE DINNER PLATES TURNED IN A DIAMOND SHAPE. NEXT IS A GOLD CHARGER, A SALAD PLATE, THEN THE FLUTED WHITE COMPOTE. THE PURPLE LINEN NAPKIN IS TUCKED UNDER THE APPETIZER PLATE. EACH GUEST'S CHAIR HOLDS EITHER COLORFUL BEADS OR ELEGANT MASKS. EVERYDAY GREEN WINE GOBLETS TEAM UP WITH GOLD-RIMMED ETCHED WATER GLASSES TO CREATE A BALANCE OF COLORS AND TEXTURES.

1

As guests mill about in the living room, they don't have to go very far for a *frosty* vodka freeze. This *tasty* drink has only three ingredients and will serve eight: a 2-liter bottle of 7UP, 12 ounces of *frozen* lemonade concentrate, thawed, and 1 pint of vodka.

2

The side *buffet* is set and ready for the serving of crab bisque. Because the table is as full and festive as a *carnival*, Ann opted to serve the soup course from her buffet, which is *delightfully* dressed in beads, masks, and garlands.

3

To help save on kitchen time, Ann picks up the appetizers of *seafood cakes* at a local restaurant, including the deliciously *rich* creole sauce that she spoons over each cake at the last minute.

2

3

FAT TUESDAY

New Orleans Vodka Freezes
with Lemon Wedges

Sun-Dried Tomato and
Goat Cheese Nachos

Seafood Cakes with Creole Sauce

Crab Bisque

Oven-Roasted Cajun Shrimp,
Corn, and Sausage with Glaze

New Orleans King Cake

Jazz Music Mandatory

*T*his menu, including the main dish, was taken from one of Ann's favorite cookbooks, *Dining by Fireflies: Unexpected Pleasures of the New South* by the Junior League of Charlotte, North Carolina. Over the years, she has adapted the recipe by the addition of summer sausage. At this particular party, Ann used 3–4 pounds of large, unpeeled gulf shrimp and eight ears of corn broken in thirds. She added an additional 2 pounds of summer sausage, sautéed until slightly browned, and then cut into bite-size slices. After boiling the corn in salted water and cooking the shrimp in a separate container of boiling spiced water, combine the shrimp, corn, and summer sausage slices in a large roasting pan. Top them with a stick of butter that has been cut into 1-inch slices.

GLAZE

Combine the following ingredients in a small bowl and pour over the shrimp, corn, and sausage just before serving.

> 1/4 cup olive oil
>
> 1/4 cup Worcestershire sauce
>
> 1/4 cup soy sauce
>
> 2 teaspoons salt
>
> 2 teaspoons pepper
>
> 2 cloves garlic, minced
>
> 2 tablespoons dried oregano
>
> Cayenne pepper to taste
>
> 1/4 teaspoon Tabasco sauce

Top with 4 lemons, cut into slices. Bake in a preheated 500 degree oven for 10 minutes, basting and turning often until the flavors are well combined and heated through. When you set this in the middle of the table, guests can help themselves and spend hours leisurely peeling and indulging in this delicious main course.

Serves 8.

Ladies' Luncheon

HERALDS SPRING'S ARRIVAL

❧

My friend Marsee Bates delights in watching nature come alive again every spring. And since she has the rare ability to make everything seem like a celebration, she decided to share her spring fever with friends by hosting a ladies' luncheon in the sunny eat-in kitchen of the fifteen-year-old traditional two-story home she shares with her husband, Mike.

Even though the weather was still too cool to dine outside, Marsee made her kitchen feel like a garden, serving the finest foods of spring on a wonderful rusted patio table. The burnished wicker chairs and refined burlap curtains that flank her tall kitchen windows add to the outdoor feel of the setting.

Featured on the menu is Marsee's famous split-pea soup. The first time I tried her soup, a group of us had decided to road-trip to Marsee's house in Wichita, Kansas, for lunch. We all share the feeling that, no matter how busy our calendars get, we have to reserve time to nurture our friendships. So we picked a date, gassed up the car, and hit the turnpike for the three-hour trip.

Marsee, who has an artist's eye, decided to add split-pea soup to her luncheon menu because it was such a lovely, creamy shade of green. She'd never made the soup before and decided to puree the peas in her blender. The plan sounded fine, until she failed to tighten the lid. She hit the puree button, then screamed in horror as mushy peas flew out of the blender and stuck to her walls. She scrambled to clean up the mess, then tried again, this time using a hand mixer in a pot to blend the peas. When we arrived, starved and ready to enjoy lunch, she told us the story of the spattered peas, and we've never let her live it down.

Pea soup looks perfect ladled into pink Depression glass sorbet cups on Marsee's luncheon table. She started collecting pink and green Depression glass after receiving her grandmother's salt and pepper cellars. For the luncheon, she weds the glass with her vintage desert rose pottery, a gift from her mother, layered atop majolica chargers. Bright linens in a pink and green floral pattern add another dash of spring color to the tabletop tableau. To brighten her guests' spirits, Marsee tucks vintage flower-seed packets atop each tower of plates. An assortment of bud vases with forsythia blooms and little snippets of fresh pea greens add a dollop of color. The ready-made quiche, a spring mix salad, and warm rolls are all you need to top off the menu. Brilliant lemon bars adorned with edible pansy blossoms give the table a burst of sun.

❧

The heart of the home is the kitchen. Preparing a table for four in the intimacy of this room can rejuvenate your spirits as much as any spring tonic. Bring nature and its colors inside, and treat your close friends to a spring luncheon that has been created just to show them how much you care. Here, this antique garden table teams up with wicker chairs and a spring color scheme to welcome the outdoors inside.

CARNATION

HUTH SEED CO., Inc.
SAN ANTONIO, TEXAS

THE OLD-FASHIONED SEED PACKETS,
USED AS PARTY FAVORS FOR THIS TABLE,
ARE SO EASY TO MAKE. SIMPLY FIND SOME
VINTAGE ARTWORK OF FLOWERS OR
VEGETABLES, MAKE ENOUGH COLOR
COPIES FOR EACH GUEST, THEN PASTE
THEM OVER THE SEED PACKETS OR SMALL

ENVELOPES YOU'VE FILLED WITH SEEDS.

LEMON DESSERT BARS, DECORATED
WITH EDIBLE FLOWER PETALS, GIVE THE
TABLE A BURST OF SUN. EDIBLE FLOWERS
ARE READILY AVAILABLE AT MOST GROCERY
STORES. IF NOT, SUBSTITUTE A FRESH SLICE
OF LEMON OR LIME.

Easter Brunch

AT THE GARRITY HOME

❦

When I was a kid, Easter was an exciting time at my house. It meant a brand-new dress to wear to Mass and baskets full of candy. And, boy, did I cash in on the candy! Since I was one of the few children on our street, neighbors who were empty-nesters brought me baskets full of candy and treats. How much better can it get for a kid?

Today, I still look forward to Easter with great excitement. Every year we invite our close friends and family over for a brunch to celebrate the beginning of spring. I'm still a kid inside, so I have to infuse this event with a touch of revelry. So, in my living room, just across from the Easter table, I hide brown farm eggs in unlikely holders, like bud vases, candlesticks, and old salt cellars. Guests of all ages have fun scouting for Easter eggs hidden in my decor.

I feel that childlike sense of excitement again as I decorate my table in light, bright colors that revive me after the long winter. I'm not one for a

Sharing special moments with dear friends reaps love and

memories that can last a lifetime.

❧

stiff, stodgy Easter table, but I still like to pull together a presentation that balances a reverence for the season with a little bit of fun.

I start by giving my dining room chairs a quick makeover. My mahogany chairs feature black leather seat cushions, but you'll rarely see them that way. With a little imagination and a few yards of fabric, I can make the dining set look brand-new. For spring, I use a light tapestry in French country blue, embellished with a ruffled skirt.

A simple table runner of striped pink ticking introduces my fresh color scheme and anchors the asymmetrical centerpiece that extends the length of my table. On one side, I select contemporary vases to display spring flowers. A candy dish holds a plump peony blossom I picked up at the florists.

Each light and layered place setting starts with a gold-rimmed charger, gold-tipped dinner plate, and salad plate. Next in the order is a candy dish filled with chocolate eggs, a take-home gift for each guest. A duo of clear glasses, each in a different style, completes each setting. Linen napkins are laced with celery green satin ribbons and a velvet pansy for a final, soft touch.

But the show-stealer on this table is the generous use of wheat grass that I discovered at the health food store. This tender, lime green grass is so succulent and brilliant, I can't resist showcasing it all over my table, as a nest for place cards, in dishes cradling eggs, in my centerpiece.

❧

THE SIDEBOARD COMPLETES THE EASTER SCENE. THIS VERSATILE PIECE OF FURNITURE IS A FAVORITE DECORATING SPOT OF MINE. I CAN'T RESIST CHANGING ITS DECOR WITH EACH SEASON AND EACH CELEBRATION. HERE, A COFFEE SERVICE AND DESSERT PLATES ARE READY TO HOLD GENEROUS SLICES OF A DREAMY COCONUT CAKE LACED WITH RASPBERRY FILLING. A PAPIER-MÂCHÉ RABBIT STANDS TALL WITH FRESH TULIPS, WHICH CONTINUE THE COLOR SCHEME FROM THE MAIN TABLE.

$\mathcal{D}$ining

UNDER THE STARS

❦

 s hosts, we draw inspiration for our social gatherings from so many sources, don't we? My friend Brenda Graves's muse for a formal dinner under the stars came from a desire to drink in the nocturnal beauty of her backyard. One night as she and her husband, Reed, relaxed on the back patio in late spring, Brenda knew she had to host a romantic twilight dinner party, with the sunset's symphony of colors as a backdrop and the early stars as a canopy.

The announcement of this spring soirée begins at the curb where Brenda fills her mailbox with wild clippings from her yard. Late spring blossoms are combined with variegated hosta leaves to welcome guests to this al fresco gathering.

Brenda is the consummate entertainer and hosts large and lavish parties in their 1920s-era two-story with a cool ease that makes me marvel. I envy her ability to relax and just enjoy what, for her, is the art of cooking.

Another reason that Brenda's parties are so successful, I think, is her careful attention to detail, whether it be her beautifully dressed dining table,

Spring turns to summer in a moment,

so on a clear moon-lit evening, use the stars as your umbrella

and drink in the romance of the evening with friends old and new.

⌘

her tantalizing cuisine, or the relaxed warmth she wraps around each of her guests. No matter how formal the event, however, by the end of the evening, we're all in Brenda's kitchen, dancing and singing!

One of my very first customers, Brenda now works at Nell Hill's. I will be forever grateful to Brenda for inviting me into her circle of friends in St. Joseph, Missouri, a town near Atchison. This fun-loving group throws the most memorable parties around. Together they have had a major influence on what has developed into the Nell Hill's style of entertaining.

Often in my decorating, I select a theme, then bring it to life through carefully chosen accessories. Brenda does the same thing to create a memorable table for her dinner under the stars.

This romantic theme is a tantalizing mix of rustic and regal. To seat her guests, she pulls a simple picnic table to the center of her flagstone patio and flanks it with weathered wooden benches and chairs. She makes the seats inviting by covering them with plump pillows, borrowed from her furniture inside.

From the star-shaped croutons on the salad to mirrored place mats that reflect the candlelight and night sky, she doesn't scrimp on one detail.

⌘

To make the table look as if it is covered with lights that fell from the sky, sprinkle tiny luminaries about. Their gleam highlights the glass and adds romance to this elegant, yet simple, table setting. Mirrors serve as place mats, catching the light given off by the shimmer of the glass and votive candles. Elegant in their simplicity, the simple blueware vases need only a relaxed arrangement of white roses and ivy. Floral arrangements should look spontaneous, not stiff and formal.

AN EDIBLE FLOWER ADORNS THIS SIMPLE SALAD MADE OF LEAFY GREENS, SPRING MIX, AND RADICCHIO. BRENDA'S MOTHER SUPPLIED THE ANTIQUE GLASS COMPOTES, DEEP ENOUGH TO USE AS SALAD BOWLS. IT IS SO EASY TO MAKE THESE CROUTONS. USING DENSE SAND-WICH BREAD AND A STAR-SHAPED COOKIE CUTTER, MARK OFF THREE STARS FOR EACH GUEST. BROWN IN A SKILLET, LIGHTLY COATED WITH BUTTER. WHILE STILL WARM, SPRINKLE WITH PARMESAN CHEESE AND LET SIT UNTIL READY TO USE. LITTLE TOUCHES LIKE FANCIFUL CROUTONS SET THE SALAD APART, YET TAKE ONLY MINUTES TO PREPARE. THE FARE SHOULD BE LIGHT AND IN KEEPING WITH SPRING OFFERINGS. A FIRST-COURSE SALAD IS FOLLOWED BY LAMB CHOPS WITH MINT JELLY, GARLIC MASHED POTATOES, AND FRESH ASPARAGUS. DESSERT SHOULD BE RICHLY DECADENT.

Backyard Shrimp Peel
Picnic in the Park
Enchanted Summer Evening
Sip and See

PART TWO

Summer

Summer's sunny weather allows us to easily entertain inside and outside, infusing all our events with the season's abundance of colorful food and dazzling decor.

There's nothing that lifts my spirits quite so high as opening my door to a beautiful, sun-kissed summer day. On a lazy Sunday afternoon, when the store is closed, I can't wait to sneak away to my garden and set up a chair amid the riot of bloom. Normally, I'm in constatnt motion.

But along with my cats, even I slow down long enough to rest for a moment in the dappled sun of our yard, enjoying the early summer breeze.

As a kid, I counted the days until school was out for the year, and we could wallow in the long and lazy days of summer. Summer evenings seemed to stretch on for infinity then, melting into twilight, when the hunt for lightning bugs began in earnest. There was something inexplicably satisfying about playing outside with your friends on a warm summer evening. There still is!

As the weather heats up, I can't wait to dazzle summer guests with a home that reflects the passion of the season. I don't make major changes, like repainting or moving furniture. Let's face it—none of us has the time or desire to remake our home four times a year. But we can achieve virtually the same effect by making small modifications in our decorating that have a huge visual impact.

Since I'm a fabric fanatic, one way I mark the changing of the seasons is through the textiles I use as accents on my furnishings. This time of year, I accessorize my off-white sofa and chairs with lightweight weaves like linen and cotton. I love

light florals and subdued stripe patterns. And I'm absolutely crazy about the classic combination of crisp white-and-black cotton (throw in a toile, and I'm in heaven). I also love to toss in bright bursts of color by mixing in some accent pillows or table linens in yummy tangerine, lemon yellow, or watermelon.

The heart of my approach to decorating is the same when it comes to entertaining. I like to build drama by layering displays, and one of my favorite techniques is to create tabletop tableaux that tell a story,

catch people off-guard, or make them smile. In summer I usually simplify my displays to showcase a few of the season's finest things.

For instance, instead of an elaborate centerpiece on my dining room table, I'll display a simple trio of ferns potted in rustic garden urns. My mantel might be graced by an unassuming line of mint julep glasses filled with zinnias from the garden. And my kitchen shelves will likely boast a display of white and cream stoneware, with my favorite picnic basket tucked in so it's ready on a moment's notice.

Once your home is dressed in its bright and breezy summer best, let the fun begin! When the weather is nice, you've just got to take the party outside on your deck, in the garden, or on your lawn.

One of my favorite spots to entertain guests is on my screened porch. I'm not one to use traditional lawn and garden furnishings and fabrics on my sheltered porch. Instead, I've filled this screened-in sanctuary with a plump upholstered chaise, an antique daybed drowning in pillows, a wooden table and chairs for small dinner parties, and a hutch I cover with my favorite treasures, like dishes, artwork, and seasonal accessories.

Having such comfortable furnishings outside lures my family onto the porch most evenings, where we listen to the hum of the cicadas and discuss the day's events. I can't tell you how many summer afternoons I've left work dreaming about grabbing a cold drink, a good book, and sinking into the chaise, only to discover that Dan and the cats have beaten me to it!

I also adore entertaining in my courtyard, a small walled garden that substitutes for a backyard. My friends Gloria and Lynda, who are master gardeners, have helped me turn this little plot of dirt into an oasis. With my brown thumb, I can't handle fussy flowers, so the courtyard's ivy-covered walls and beds of easy-care perennials are perfect for me.

Through the years I've filled my garden with things I love, like a birdbath filled with amber glass stones that dance with the summer light and large iron urns filled with flowering vines.

Casual backyard barbecues definitely have their place. Every year on Father's Day, I host a small gathering for Dan and serve his favorite steaks. But, usually, when I entertain in my courtyard, I like to do it up big. The heart of the Nell Hill's style of decorating is mixing objects of great value with things that are more ordinary. No place is this zany mixed-up style more intriguing and effective than in summer outdoor entertaining.

People think I'm crazy when I bring out my best china and crystal, fine linens, and silver for garden dinners. I know it's daring and a bit unconventional to set a lavish table on a brick patio, but I can't resist because it's an absolutely luxurious experience to dine in high style under the stars.

I love to hear the inventive ways my friends and customers artfully blend the rustic and refined in their summer entertaining. On the next few pages, I will take you to a few wonderful summer celebrations held at the homes of some good friends. The parties featured here range from beautifully grand to refreshingly simple. I hope they will inspire you to host a gathering of your own and make the most of the marvelous months of summer.

❧

I start the celebration inside for Father's Day—Dan's favorite cocktail is a cold beer with pistachios.

Backyard

SHRIMP PEEL AND SUSHI PARTY

❧

June is my favorite month for outdoor entertaining in the Midwest. The weather is sublime—not too hot, not too cold—and the soft twilight hours seem to stretch on forever. That's the time of year I start hinting for an invitation from my friends Ann and Guy Humphreys, the reigning king and queen of impromptu patio parties. The Humphreys are warm and relaxed hosts who make you feel like family the moment you walk in their door. I've spent many a delightful summer night on their patio, enjoying the fine fare and even finer company.

Thanks to their carefully thought-out landscaping, the patio is a cool and inviting retreat, even on hot days. Towering trees provide filtered shade, while blooming understory trees, like redbuds and crab apples, lend privacy from the golf course that adjoins their yard.

The garden terrace that overlooks the golf course provides a perfect backdrop for this simple gathering. You know it is going to be special the minute you spot the chandeliers hanging from the tree branches. This patio was designed with an ample supply of electrical outlets, so hanging chandeliers outside requires only a stepladder and s-hooks. Just dangle these exquisite lights from sturdy branches around the patio. As early twilight falls, a romantic light descends over the party. The sparkle of the crystal prisms are dramatic and unexpected in a garden setting, along with the romantic addition of the large pillar candles perched close by.

The back patio of their brick ranch was designed with this kind of entertaining in mind. Instead of laying a featureless slab of concrete, their large brick and flagstone terrace is artfully divided into smaller, more intimate areas. They've invested in a number of similar wrought-iron dining sets so even when they host large gatherings, guests can cluster into smaller groups to enjoy drinks, dinner, and lively conversation.

Ann fills her planters with easy-care annuals like white periwinkles, which almost glow in the late dusky hours. And a luxurious bed of ivy, which creeps up the house's brick walls, tree trunks, and everything else that doesn't move, provides a soothing backdrop for festive outdoor affairs.

This shrimp and sushi cocktail party is as easy as boiling water. Once you've cooked and chilled the shrimp and picked up sushi from your favorite restaurant or market, all that's left is icing down an assortment of long-neck bottles of beer.

When the sun goes down, the lights go up, and sometimes the cocktail party evolves into a late dinner. This neighborhood throws a last-minute potluck supper without missing a beat. One of the parties they remember most fondly was a night when everyone went home and brought what they had in the refrigerator back to the Humphreys. It shows that when you're properly prepared with the essentials, a last-minute party can be the best party.

Impromptu gatherings on a well-designed patio can be as relaxing for the hostess as they are for the guests. Have the necessities on hand to pull it off with style.

❧

INVEST IN THE BASIC TOOLS YOU NEED TO HOST LARGE GET-TOGETHERS, LIKE SERVING PIECES, TABLEWARE, AND TABLE LINENS. COLLECT CASUAL STONEWARE AND FORMAL CHINA THAT YOU CAN MIX AND MATCH TO CREATE VISUAL INTEREST ON THE TABLE. WHEN PLANNING YOUR BACKYARD PATIO, DECKS, AND PORCHES, WIRE FOR OUTSIDE LIGHTING. WITH THIS STOREHOUSE OF PARTY WARE AT YOUR FINGERTIPS, YOU'LL BE ABLE TO ENTERTAIN AT A MOMENT'S NOTICE WHEN FRIENDS ARRIVE ON YOUR DOORSTEP LOOKING FOR FUN.

THIS TABLE CONTINUES THE THEME WITH PINK GERBER DAISIES. THE DEEP GREEN COLOR OF THE EDAMAME APPETIZERS OFFERS AN EXPLOSION OF COLOR. GUESTS CAN EASILY GRAB AN ICED BEER, COOLED IN METAL URNS STOLEN FROM THE GARDEN, THEN MIX AND MINGLE AROUND THE ENTIRE GARDEN ROOM.

Picnic

IN THE PARK

Don't scrimp on style and elegance when dining in the park.

Make your picnic spread a showstopper that's as fine

as any indoor dining experience.

What would summer be without a picnic? I love to pack a meal and escape to the park, lake, or outdoor concert. And when I do, I take the romance with me. Instead of using practical plastic plates and silverware, I fill my basket with my finest—china, silver, crystal, fine linens, and even an iron candelabra for oh-so-romantic lighting.

For a picnic blanket, I pull a thick quilt off the bed. I also bring along some plump pillows from the couch so when my guests and I have eaten our fill, we can lounge comfortably under the stars.

A picnic can be easy and elegant and should never involve compli-
cated food preparation. Wouldn't that defeat the purpose of relaxing in the
park? I'm not a cook, so for me, picnics start with a trip to the local deli, where
I grab chicken salad sandwiches, a colorful salad drowning in summer berries,
and a mouthwatering meringue pie.

I toss out the standard to-go packaging of Styrofoam and plastic and
serve my movable feast in style. Instead of boring plastic baggies, I'll wrap each
sandwich in festive paper tied up with a gingham ribbon. Depending on my
mood, I'll serve the side dishes in a playful stoneware bowl or on an elegant
silver platter. And I'll commandeer a fun caddy from the kitchen shelves to
hold condiments and silverware.

Picnics are so fabulous because once the initial planning and packing
are done, you're free to simply relax and soak up the sun. My favorite picnic
menu is "to go" food—most of my energy goes into making outdoor escapades
luxurious and comfortable.

This *colorful* berry salad, drizzled with poppy seed dressing, and topped with slivered almonds, shows off the season's *best* berries. Blackberries, strawberries, and raspberries are *bursting* with color, crunch, and flavor, doing their part to add to a perfect summer solstice.

This lemon pie from a local restaurant has the most *alluring* cloud of meringue topping ever seen. Why should you try to top that one? Leave the baking to the pros, then spend the time you saved *frolicking* in the sun.

This handy caddy filled with mason jars holds the picnic *essentials*: silverware, crunchy pickles, celery sticks, carrots, and even a few blooms tucked in just for *fun*.

2

3

ENCHANTED

Summer Evening

A weathered garden bust encircled in a wreath, soft candlelight,

and heirloom crystal partner to create an unforgettable party

and an enchanting summer evening for those lucky enough to land here.

❧

When I receive an invitation for a dinner party at the home of Brenda and Reed Graves, I get positively giddy. Whether Brenda is entertaining formally in her sensational dining room, which is filled with vintage crystal and heirloom silver, or casually in her sunny kitchen, I know I'm in for a culinary treat. But recently, I got to enjoy a dinner at Brenda's that was like no other: an Italian feast served al fresco.

Since Brenda is the third generation to live in this home, built by her grandfather, she knows every nook and cranny. The venue for this event, however, was an area she has rarely used for entertaining: the flagstone courtyard situated on the side of her house. Shaded by the most enormous pin oak I've ever seen and cooled by a gentle north breeze, Brenda knew this forgotten courtyard was the ideal place for a summer dinner spotlighting a traditional Italian dish she was dying to make: timpano.

When Brenda throws a party, she likes her menu and decorations to revolve around a theme. She has a knack for selecting themes that are inventive and fun, not silly or trite. The idea for the timpano dinner party came to her as she watched a movie that featured the dish. With a minimum of research, she came up with the recipe. An accomplished chef, Brenda decided she just had to make this hearty meal for friends, and an outdoor dinner party with a rustic Italian twist was born.

When most of us entertain large groups, we're stuck with the age-old dilemma of where to seat everyone. Most of us don't have huge tables—especially outside—so we have to be inventive. Here's a trick we use at Nell Hill's, and one that Brenda relies on to accommodate guests at her outdoor events.

To seat large groups at my parties, I rely on folding chairs made from bamboo or other natural materials—they look beautiful and store away easily between events. Or, you can elevate the look of the event by bringing your formal dining chairs outside for the party.

On the following pages, you'll see how Brenda artfully brought elegant refinement to her rustic patio through a beautifully appointed table, resplendent in her grandmother's crystal, china, and silver. You'll also find her tantalizing menu and tips for presenting the delicious cuisine for guests.

❧

Bottles of red wine, normally served at room temperature, are briefly chilled in a wooden dough board so the wine isn't too warm when it's transferred to the table.

PURCHASE A SHEET OF PLYWOOD AND HAVE IT CUT INTO THE TABLE LENGTH YOU DESIRE. BRENDA HAS THREE DIFFERENT PLYWOOD TABLETOPS STORED IN HER GARAGE, EACH A DIFFERENT SHAPE AND SIZE, SO SHE CAN HOST DINNER PARTIES OF VARYING SIZES.

NEXT, SECURE YOUR PLYWOOD TABLETOP TO THE BASES OF INEXPENSIVE ALUMINUM OUTDOOR TABLES. IF YOU HAVE EVEN MORE SUBSTANTIAL PEDESTAL BASES ON HAND, USE THOSE. YOU CAN ALSO HAVE THE PLYWOOD CUT TO EXTEND OVER THE SIDES OF SMALLER TABLES, IF THEY ARE HEAVY ENOUGH TO BALANCE THE OVERHANG. THIS ENLARGES THE TABLE ENOUGH TO PROVIDE ROOMY SEATING.

FINALLY, COVER YOUR AD HOC TABLE WITH A FLOOR-LENGTH TABLE-CLOTH SO IT LOOKS LIKE A BEAUTIFUL BANQUET TABLE. AT NELL HILL'S, WE SUGGEST USING A LARGE TABLECLOTH MADE FROM A DURABLE FABRIC LIKE HEAVY LINEN OR DUCK CLOTH. THEN, LAYER MORE ELEGANT TABLECLOTHS ON TOP TO ADD FINESSE AND A FINISHED LOOK. IN THIS SETTING, WE ALSO LAYERED IN PAISLEY THROWS.

Timpano is one of many different and substantial pasta dishes that could be the entree for this Italian feast. Timpano is prepared in a large oven-safe bowl that is filled with pasta, hard-boiled eggs, and meatballs with layers of red sauce in between. A crust is baked over the top of the bowl and, after baking, the bowl is inverted. When cooled, simply slice through the colorful, delicious layers and serve this beautiful dish as your main course.

Pique guests' appetites with an incredible assortment of cheeses, gourmet crackers, salamis, and colorful condiments. The antipasto platters stand ready on the brick wall of this backyard fireplace, which has been transformed into an inviting buffet. If Brenda is well-known for any one dish, it might be her heirloom tomato salad, layered with fresh mozzarella and homegrown basil pesto. It makes a tasty, visually satisfying salad presentation. The evening is topped off with a light, colorful lemon biscotti cheesecake and assorted dessert wines.

꧁꧂

The trick to re-creating this memorable evening is infusing the presentation with drama. Brown wicker chargers hold elegant silver trays that don't match but are approximately the same size and style. Next are colorful stoneware plates that bear the image of a bird. The cream-colored cut-lace linens, alongside the gold-rimmed crystal and the silver service, add consistency and balance to this textured tabletop arrangement.

Stoneware 1 plates, pitch pots, imported olives, fresh fruit, and creamy yellow cheeses entice guests to munch and *mingle* around the antipasto assortment.

This antique *pitcher* 2 holds one of the few floral arrangements found at this party. Simple stems of Japanese *iris* hold their own here.

The hearty meal is topped off with this special *lemon* 3 biscotti cheesecake, served with coffees and dessert wines. The lemon curd topping is both sweet and tart, and provides the *perfect* complement to the light, creamy filling of the cake. The buttery crumbs melt in your mouth.

2
3

MENU

SUMMER FEAST

———————

Antipasto Platter with Assortment
of Salamis, Cheeses, Olives, Peppers, Crackers,
and Bread Sticks

Layered Heirloom Tomato Salad

Timpano or Hearty Pasta Noodle Main Dish
such as Lasagna or Manicotti

Crusty Italian Breads with
Dipping Oils and Butter

Lemon Biscotti Cheesecake

Assortment of Italian Wines

Coffee

LAYERED HEIRLOOM TOMATO SALAD

TAPENADE

   2 cups pitted Kalamata olives

   4 garlic cloves

   4 anchovy fillets

   2 tablespoons pine nuts

   1/2 cup olive oil

   Salt and pepper to taste

Blend the olives, garlic, anchovies, and pine nuts in a food processor until almost smooth. With the machine running, add the oil; process until blended. Season with the salt and pepper. (This can be made 2 days ahead, covered, and chilled.)

DRESSING

   1/4 cup white wine vinegar

   2 tablespoons honey

   1 tablespoon Dijon mustard

   3/4 cup olive oil

   12 large fresh basil leaves, thinly sliced

   Salt and pepper to taste

Whisk the vinegar, honey, and mustard in a bowl. Gradually whisk in the oil. Stir in the basil. Season with salt and pepper. (This can be made 8 hours ahead. Let stand at room temperature.)

SALAD

   8 to 10 large tomatoes, preferably heirloom tomatoes of assorted colors, each cut crosswise into 1/2-inch slices

   Two 8-ounce balls drained freshwater-packed mozzarella, cut into 1/3-inch rounds

Place one tomato slice on each of eight plates. Spread each with generous portion of tapenade; top with one mozzarella round. Repeat the layering. Top each stack with a third tomato slice. Chop the remaining tomato slices. Place the chopped tomatoes in a bowl with 2 tablespoons of the dressing. Spoon this mixture over the top of each serving.

Serves 8.

Sip and See

TO WELCOME NEW BABY

❧

Have you noticed how silly we act when we're talking to a baby? Our voices rise two octaves and we don the most hilarious expressions, trying to coax a smile from the darling bundle. Now, imagine a room full of doting "aunties" cooing over the baby they've pined for these nine long months, and you have a good idea of what Barb Fricke's Sip and See is like.

A Sip and See is a wonderful tradition to establish and a special way for friends, family, and neighbors to gather together to welcome a precious new baby that's come into their lives. At this afternoon gathering, Barb, her daughter Erin, and her granddaughter Katelyn host a party for their dear friend and neighbor Joyce Colman. This "Sip and See" gathering will welcome Joyce's new grandbaby, Ella Kate, and her mother, Stephanie. For baby Ella Kate's grand debut, Barb dresses her 1923 Tudor home in the soft and sweet colors of a baby's nursery.

Layer by layer, Barb gives the table character, starting with the floral tablecloth in gold, pink, mint, and lavender. Antique silver baby cups make ideal vases for a spray of pink and cream flowers.

Sometimes spontaneously dressed tables can be the most memorable. The instant Barb saw the elegantly wrapped baby gifts, each a piece of art ensconced in charming vintage papers, she knew they were as pretty as any centerpiece, so she quickly incorporated the parcels into her table decorations.

While party guests get a chance to hold Ella Kate, share sage advice with the new mom, and tell stories about their own children, they enjoy delicious fare. The buffet is dressed with a wide array of tasty treats from aromatic baked Brie and prosciutto-wrapped asparagus, to petit fours and snowy white cupcakes topped with tiny sugared violets.

The height of the centerpiece adds the
needed *drama* to the scene, and a special
angel watches over the day's activities.

Everyone gets a chance to hold baby Ella Kate,
even the littlest one, Katelyn. Her grandma
chose this *summer* polka dot dress to coor-
dinate with the napkins tucked inside the glass
mugs that stand ready for *guests*.

Family *baby* photos are mixed in with the
food to carry the party theme over to the
lavish buffet of finger foods. Only a mom
could prepare all of her *daughter's*
favorite cocktail foods—a special
indulgence for a new mom who needs a
little tender, loving care.

Fall Mini-Fete
Halloween
Thanksgiving Table
A Chocolate Gathering

PART THREE

Autumn

In this season of gratitude, let your closest friends know how much you appreciate them by hosting memorable events that pay tribute to fall and friendship.

❦

As the oppressive heat and humidity of late summer begin to melt into the light and crisp days of autumn, I feel reenergized. By far, this is my favorite time of year. The trees along the Missouri River burn red, orange, and yellow, and the surrounding farms are rich with golden grain.

The local college bustles

with activity, area fall festivals draw guests from far and wide, and friends pour into Nell Hill's to get a jump on their holiday shopping.

I have an extra bounce in my step as I ready my home to receive guests for the holidays, whether they are friends coming for dinner, pint-sized ghosts and goblins scouting for candy, or family members ready for a Thanksgiving feast.

Perhaps one of the reasons I'm enthralled with fall is that I have so much fun weaving the natural beauty of the season into my interior decorating. Fall's many hues of sage green, rusty red, chestnut brown, and rich gold are among my absolute favorites, and I can't resist using this color palette year-round in my decorating (and in my wardrobe). Since my home is done in warm neutrals, it's easy for me to bring in the fabulous colors of fall and showcase the season's natural beauty in my decor. So, even before the air turns cool, I get impatient to fill my home with all that fall has to offer.

To give my creamy white sofa a new look for fall, I just toss in a paisley throw of cinnabar and ocher, or add a few plump pillows in menswear fabric. The table goes through a quick transformation when I bring out amber goblets, a perennial favorite that I use year-round when entertaining. And I can't resist using the bounty of the land—gourds, pumpkins, and luminous fall foliage. You'll find all of these tucked into my decor in some of the most unusual places.

I always set the mood at the front door, giving guests a glimpse of the seasonal delights that await them inside. Through the years, I've had lots of fun experimenting with the exterior door, dressing it up with all manner of unlikely items, like china plates and mirrors. But my favorite front-door treatment so far is an oil still life in an opulent golden frame, nested in artificial fall berries, leaves, and vines.

Inside the foyer, I fill a bentwood urn with leggy branches from the yard, mixing in beautiful boughs of faux fall foliage and berries. I like to use lifelike artificial greenery so I don't have to worry about leaves or sap landing on area rugs.

At the local pumpkin patch or produce stand, I stock up on pumpkins, gourds, red apples, and pears, which are among the cornerstones of my autumn decorations. It's fun to use these inexpensive treasures in inventive ways. I top a weathered cement pillar with a portly pumpkin, elegantly displayed on a silver plate, protected under an etched cloche. Tuck a handful of tiny pumpkins into a tabletop tableau of tin cups and candlesticks. Cascade tendrils of fall berries from the top of a bookcase or armoire.

Because I like to entertain both outside and inside during the fall, I want the front porch and garden to be as fun and inviting as my home's interior. On the front porch, I tie up the stately boxwood topiaries that flank my door with a bright Halloween ribbon. For an added burst of color, I add a pumpkin or two. In the courtyard, I top a trio of iron pillars with fat gourds. To create mysterious lighting in the garden, I hang rustic lanterns in the trees

As soon as my home is bursting with the bounty of this marvelous season, I'm on the phone, inviting friends over to help celebrate the arrival of autumn.

Fall Mini-Fete

IN THE GARDEN

❧

The days are just starting to get shorter and cooler, and it won't be long before your holiday "to-do" list gets longer. It's the perfect time to host a quiet evening together with your closest friends, enjoying a long, leisurely dinner in your garden. I love to entertain outside during the crisp, clear, moonlit autumnal evenings.

Before the harvest moon lights up the night sky, I serve wine, cheese, and crisp apples on a side bench in my garden, inviting guests to mill about, catching up with one another before we are seated for our first course.

Whether I'm entertaining two or twenty guests, I like to create a feeling of intimacy at my dinner parties. So for this early-fall party, I set up a table for four under the arch of an iron gazebo. To make the gazebo feel like a cozy room, I hang a black lantern, ensconced in honeysuckle vine and fall berries, from the top.

Lanterns tucked throughout the garden add romance and intrigue as darkness falls.

❧

To help build drama at this courtyard dinner, I unearth my favorite garden staples, like a weathered urn or a worn birdbath, and give them an entirely new use. A piece of crumbling garden statuary when placed atop a table is a wonderful beginning for a memorable centerpiece, and rusted finials become unusual place-card holders.

Instead of a linen tablecloth, for this fall fete I covered the table with a sheet of moss, cut to fit the tabletop. I inserted festive fall napkins into small cornucopias and served the first course in a bowl made from a gourd, which was kept hot under a glass cloche.

❧

If you look closely at the tabletop in this setting, you'll see that instead of a traditional table-cloth, I used a bed of moss. The earthy table covering was easy to make. I purchased the moss in a large roll at my favorite garden store, then cut it in a circle the size of my tabletop.

Appetizers reflecting the season's bounty are offered on this side bench in the garden. A crisp wine served with cheese and sweet apple slices makes for a perfect beginning. When your guests arrive, surprise them with a hostess gift—something that they can take away to remember this evening and your special friendship.

MENU

FALL MINI-FETE

SELECTED SEASONAL APPLES: FUJI, JONAGOLD, GOLDEN
DELICIOUS, OR MCINTOSH

RICH CHEESES: NEW YORK SHARP CHEDDAR,
MAYTAG BLUE CHEESE, OR STILTON

CRISP, FRUITY WHITE WINE, CHILLED IMPORTED BEERS,
SPARKING WATER AND LIME SLICES

CREAM OF RED POTATO AND ROSEMARY SOUP

FIELD GREENS WITH GOAT CHEESE AND BALSAMIC
VINAIGRETTE GARNISHED WITH ANY OF THE FOLLOWING:
WALNUTS, DRIED CRANBERRIES, OR SLICED PEARS

ROASTED PORK LOIN OR GRILLED PORK TENDERLOIN

WILD RICE WITH MUSHROOMS SAUTÉED IN OLIVE OIL
AND SPRINKLED WITH SHREDDED PARMESAN CHEESE

PEAR OR APPLE TART SERVED WITH VANILLA ICE CREAM

CREAM OF RED POTATO AND ROSEMARY SOUP

*T*his recipe is our favorite from Cheryll Hartell, chef at The Vineyard's Fine Dining Restaurant in Weston, Missouri.

❧

Boil the potatoes until tender, cool, and chop all ingredients ahead of time for quick "à la minute" preparation.

   1 tablespoon butter

   1 tablespoon flour

   1 quart heavy cream

   1½ pounds baby red potatoes,
       boiled and diced

   ½ cup diced red bell pepper

   ½ cup diced red onion

   ¼ cup chopped scallions or chives

   1 tablespoon finely chopped rosemary

   Salt and pepper to taste

GARNISH

   Shavings of Parmesan
      or Romano cheese

   Crème fraiche or sour cream

   Diced peppers and onions

   Fresh sprigs of rosemary

Over low heat, melt the butter in a deep saucepan and whisk in the flour. Add the cream and whisk to ensure the flour mixture is dissolved in the cream. Add the potatoes, red pepper, red onion, scallions, and rosemary. Increase the heat to medium and stir occasionally until thick and creamy. Garnish each serving with cheese shavings, crème fraiche or sour cream, diced peppers, and a bit of onions and a fresh sprig of rosemary. Serve with an assortment of lavash crackers and hot crusty bread.

Serves 4.

 Halloween
ISN'T JUST FOR KIDS

❦

No longer just for kids, Halloween has become one of the biggest events of the year for retailers. During this spooky celebration, grown-ups are given permission to pretend for a day, donning costumes, playing pranks, and attending parties.

Halloween is especially big in Atchison, which has been dubbed the most haunted town in Kansas. To celebrate our town's ghostly heritage, I like to decorate my 130-year-old home with spooky sophistication. In the weeks just before Halloween, I modify my fall decor by adding scary details that appeal to kids and adults. For instance, the black exterior door boasts a beveled mirror that creates fun-house distortions of visitors waiting to be ushered in.

❦

ONCE INSIDE, GUESTS HELP
THEMSELVES TO HOT SPICED CIDER,
SERVED ON THE BUFFET IN THE DINING
ROOM. THE TRADITIONAL SILVER TEA
SERVICE GETS A TERRIFYING TWEAK
WHEN IT IS MIXED IN WITH AN IMPOSING
SILVER CANDELABRA, BLACK PILLAR
CANDLES, AND A STUFFED RAVEN THAT
WOULD EVEN SCARE EDGAR ALLAN POE.
THE ARTWORK CHOSEN TO HANG OVER
THIS SIDE SERVICE ENHANCES THE DRAMA
OF THE SCENE BELOW.

*T*HINK LIKE A KID AGAIN BY ADDING SMALL
TOUCHES TO YOUR DINING ROOM TABLE AND
BUFFET THAT TEMPORARILY MAKE YOUR FALL
DECOR A BIT MORE SINISTER.

A SET OF GOTHIC BLACK CAKE PLATES
MAKE PERFECT RISERS FOR BOUQUETS OF
ORANGE ROSES, VINTAGE HALLOWEEN
FIGURINES, AND GOURDS DUSTED IN
GLITTER. BRIGHTLY POLISHED SILVER
SERVERS AND CANDELABRA ADD SPARKLE TO
THIS MENACING SELECTION OF ACCESSORIES.

THE BACKS OF THE DINING
ROOM CHAIRS ARE SHROUDED IN
A FEW YARDS OF SCRIM TIED WITH

A PLAYFUL BLACK AND ORANGE
RIBBON, ECHOING THE THEME
FROM THE FRONT DOOR.

AT THIS PARTY, THE ADULTS WILL BEG
TO BE SEATED AT THE KIDS' TABLE, SET UP
ON THE SCREENED PORCH SO THAT PINT-
SIZED PARTY GUESTS CAN GIGGLE AS LOUDLY
AS THEY WANT. THE TABLE IS COVERED IN A
WASHABLE BLACK-AND-WHITE PLAID QUILT.
ORANGE PLACEMATS ARE THEN TOPPED
WITH BLACK AND WHITE TRANSFERWARE.
AMBER GOBLETS HOLD CHECKED NAPKINS.
BUT THE CROWNING GLORY IS ON TOP OF
THE TOWER OF DISHES: PAPIER-MÂCHÉ
PUMPKIN BASKETS FILLED WITH SWEETS
FOR THE CHILDREN TO TAKE HOME. THE
COOKIES SHAPED LIKE GHOSTS, BLACK CATS,
CRESCENT MOONS, AND MASKED PUMPKINS
ARE IRRESISTIBLE FOR KIDS OF ALL AGES.
WITH THESE TREAT BASKETS, NO NEED TO
WORRY ABOUT THE MAIN COURSE.

Thanksgiving Table

ELEGANCE AND STYLE AT
THE GARRITY HOME

❧

Call me crazy, but I love to host my family's Thanksgiving feast every year. Dan and I split duties—he does all the cooking, and I do all the decorating. As he bangs about in the kitchen, basting the turkey and mashing the potatoes, I am busy creating a table that will show those who are dearest to me just how much I love them.

I learned from my mother-in-law, Mimi, that one of the best ways we can honor our guests is to invest the time necessary to create a superlative dining table for important holiday meals. It's in her memory every year that I try to make my Thanksgiving table simply stunning.

The scene is nearly set, thanks to my advanced fall decorating. Now, all I have to do is add those special touches that help embody my feeling of thankfulness. What better way to illustrate how much we truly have than by measuring our bounty? So, I decided to actually use an old scale as part of my centerpiece, piling each side high with fruits, flowers, and gourds displayed in silver and crystal containers.

Each place setting contains sumptuous layers of rust, sage, and amber. I started with a rich paisley throw, turned on the diagonal. Beaded silver chargers, crisp white linens, and leaf-shaped salad plates create a base for a spray of fall berries and a candy dish holding a perfect, plump pear.

On such formal occasions, I like to include a beautifully written menu card and place card at each place setting. This lovely series was created by my friend Marsee and features vintage drawings from old bookplates.

On the buffet, I carried on the theme, incorporating a fabulous brass scale into my display. I added other fall flourishes, like sunflowers in a terracotta urn and an empty bird's nest in a golden goblet.

A Chocolate Gathering

AN AFTER-SHOPPING PARTY WITH FRIENDS

This chocolate buffet is as much a feast for the eyes

as it is for the mouth. The mix of colors, textures, shapes,

and sizes make this sweet meal a masterpiece.

∽

If my friend Marsee had any say in it, chocolate would be declared one of the four major food groups. Her passion for rich, creamy chocolate is matched by her desire to spend time with friends and by her zeal for shopping.

Through a stroke of genius, Marsee decided to combine these three favorite pastimes into one fun holiday event. Early in the holiday season, right after Thanksgiving, she and a gaggle of girlfriends conspired to spend a day together, shopping for everyone on their gift list. Then, the footsore and happy band of shoppers made their way to Marsee's house to revive themselves with a decadent chocolate feast.

Guests gathered in Marsee's living room and relaxed with a steaming mug of hot cocoa and frothy whipped cream, spiced with a cinnamon stick, and nibbling on melt-in-your-mouth chocolate confections. For the health conscious in the crowd, she added tasty finger sandwiches of prosciutto, shaved Romano cheese, and watercress on herbed rolls.

Like most of us, Marsee is very busy with work, home, and community commitments. So she's come up with a time-saving mantra that spares her the headache of trying to do it all when she entertains: Presentation over preparation. For instance, for her chocolate gathering, Marsee picked up many of the chocolate dishes

Marsee's Mantra: "Presentation over Preparation."

at the bakery and confections shop. That allows her to spend less time in the kitchen and more time doing what she enjoys most—creating a showstopping display of food that is as enchanting as the delicacies on the plates.

I like to be inventive when I come up with spots to display the food for a gathering, like the time I served appetizers on my porch rail. That's why I loved how Marsee set up her luncheon service on her baby grand piano. She draped a luxurious throw to protect the wood and add rich texture to her display.

Entertaining should be as much fun for you as for your guests. I know Marsee felt like a kid at the grocery store filling her shopping cart

with cookies, chocolate-dipped strawberries and apricots, bonbons, and dozens of other rich confections.

To show off the treats, give them a spot at center stage, using a variety of cake plates stacked in stunning tiers, each rimmed with new and different delicacies. Crystal cups, silver vases, sorbet glasses—all were shined up and invited to the party to hold the banquet of chocolate.

As guests departed, Marsee gave them a delightful hostess gift— a bronze box tied up with a silver ribbon, filled with luxury spa items like scented lotions and bath salts, so they could relax in a hot tub after a satisfying day of shopping, laughing, and eating the season's most decadent fare.

Christmas Eve Supper
Christmas Morning
Christmas Day
New Year's Eve
Valentine's Day

PART FOUR

Winter

No matter what holiday traditions we honor in our homes,

it is the peaceful times spent with family and

close friends that are most important.

❧

OUTSIDE MY FROSTED WINDOWS, THE SNOW SWIRLS ABOUT, COVER-

ING MY GARDEN IN A PRISTINE BLANKET OF WHITE. BUT INSIDE, CUDDLED

UP ON THE SOFA BY A ROARING FIRE, I'M WARM AND COZY, FRANTICALLY

FILLING A LEGAL PAD WITH A LIST OF THINGS I HAVE TO DO DURING THE

BUSY HOLIDAY SEASON.

Even though things can get hectic, I absolutely love the holidays. From the opulent decorations that fill our homes inside and out, to the tantalizing smells of cinnamon, pine, and fresh-baked sugar cookies, the season fills our senses (and our stomachs—I can't keep my hands off decadent foods like fudge and eggnog).

But most of all, I love the plethora of parties, dinners, and special events that fill the calendar this time of year. The holidays bring rich traditions and happy reunions, and all year long I look forward to entertaining during this season of celebration.

Whether it is a grand Christmas dinner or a small luncheon for friends, I can't seem to get enough of food, friends, and fun during the holidays. But before I open my door to bands of merrymakers, I first make my home a visual feast that delights all who enter.

Every year I like to experiment with my holiday decorations, retiring tired trims and infusing my displays with fun, new baubles, and greens. I firmly believe there is no one right way to decorate for the holidays. Some people like to do it up big, while others strive for a sparse and simple look. Depending on my mood and schedule, I've decorated both ways. But while my holiday decor changes year to year, I hold fast to the decorative details that have become the cornerstone of the Nell Hill's Christmas look.

The first step to making your home gorgeous for the holidays is to go gaga over greens. Beautiful garlands, individual flower stems, and swags create a necessary backdrop for all your other decorations, and without them, even the most magnificent display looks flat.

For years I would use nothing but real pine in my decorating, but now I've switched to faux garlands. Today's fakes are absolutely gorgeous, and they don't ooze sap or drop sticky needles. I can't resist the wide variety of greens available today, from the feathery, frost-covered pine boughs to boxwood branches that look as if they've been wilted by the first frost. But my favorites are the traditional twists of evergreen, which I loosely loop on my banister, through doorways, on my chandeliers, and over my mantel.

Another Nell Hill's decorating secret is to display your Christmas tree in a garden urn instead of a traditional stand. The idea for this unusual tree stand hit me a few years ago,

after our Christmas tree crashed to the ground during a dinner party, nearly knocking Dan out. I knew I had to come up with an alternative to the traditional but unstable thumbscrew stand, so on a whim, I stuck our tree in a garden urn and fell in love with the look. Urns not only give trees added height and majesty, they look marvelous even when they aren't surrounded by gifts. And because they elevate the tree a foot or two off the ground, they provide much-needed floor space.

The third ingredient of the Nell Hill's Christmas look is to make your home luminescent with candlelight. The soft luster gives warmth and adds depth and texture to all your holiday decorations. This time of year, I buy votives by the boxload to use throughout the house. I brighten the entryway by hanging glass votive cups from the twists of greens, branches, and rich ribbons that wind down the banister. A cluster of candles on the dining table makes the room positively glow. And I have to have candles on the mantel to give my living room a feeling of peace and serenity.

At Nell Hill's we also relish the challenge of finding new uses for familiar items. For instance, instead of just hanging beautiful glass ornaments on the tree, I use them to decorate the entire house. You'll find bulbs poured in a glass apothecary jar, pooled around a candle in a hurricane, adding color to twists of greenery, and cascading from chandeliers. Conversely, I enjoy using ordinary objects to trim the tree, like paper lanterns or a collection of vintage hand mirrors.

Finally, don't forget to have a little fun with your holiday decor. While I dress most of my home in sophisticated splendor this time of year, I like to decorate the kitchen with bright and whimsical accessories. I'm a nut for black and white, and used this color combination as the inspiration for my holiday kitchen. Who would expect to find darling creamers suspended by cheery ribbons from a kitchen light fixture or transferware plates hung inside wreaths in my kitchen window?

Christmas Eve Supper

IN SILVER, RED, AND WHITE

❧

When I was growing up, my family owned a clothing store, so the Christmas season started early for us. But the celebration truly began on Christmas Eve, when we closed up the shop and gathered with employees and their families to toast the season.

Christmas is steeped in time-honored conventions, and if we change or leave out one of our family's favorite customs, the cries of protest can be heard from young and old alike. But my friend Marsee has found a way to artfully infuse her family's traditions with fun, new ideas so their holiday gatherings never get stale.

A sentimental soul, Marsee treasures her past and has carried on many of her mother's practices at the holidays. One of her favorites is Christmas Eve dinner, which doubles as a romantic anniversary celebration for her parents.

All the restaurants in the small Kansas town where Marsee grew up were closed on Christmas Eve, so Marsee's parents could never go out on the town to

celebrate their wedding anniversary. Instead, Marsee's mother used her considerable skills as an entertainer to create a magical and romantic dinner at their home. When Marsee and her brother both married within days of Christmas, the traditional anniversary celebration on Christmas Eve became a family affair.

Marsee always puts a great deal of time and effort into decorating for guests, and one peek at her dining table proves her Christmas Eve celebration is no exception. The magnificently set table blends vintage Christmas decorations and wedding keepsakes. Her parents' wedding cake topper served as the inspiration piece for the table, dictating the color scheme and tone of the display.

At her table, as in her life, Marsee weds her family's heirlooms with those of her husband's. Each place setting begins with a contemporary white charger holding a silver tray. White Haviland dinner plates and ornate pearl-handled silverware passed down from Mike's ancestors blend perfectly with Marsee's mother's china. A red napkin contrasts with the clear Depression glass plates, china, and heirloom crystal. Elegant Christmas poppers, another family tradition, complete this charming arrangement.

After a *lively* dinner, the family enjoys a rich

dessert of flourless chocolate cake served on

the dining room sideboard. *Happy* and

full, they adjourn to the living room, where

they sit by the *fireplace* and read a

Christmas story aloud.

Presented in a rounded *silver* dome, this

savory main course gets the notice it deserves:

A *traditional* beef tenderloin, marinated

in oil, rosemary, and garlic and *adorned*

with aromatic rosemary branches, is laced

with garlic-roasted red potatoes.

MENU

CHRISTMAS EVE SUPPER

Fruit Cup of Bing Cherries, Blood Oranges,
and Pomegranate Seeds Laced with Sweet
Champagne or Cranberry Juice

Red and Green Vegetable Medley
of Red Cherry Tomatoes,
Snap Peas, and Asparagus

Garlic-Roasted Red Potatoes

Beef Tenderloin Marinated in
Olive Oil, Rosemary, and Garlic

Flourless Chocolate Cake,
Coffee, and Assorted
After-Dinner Liqueurs

FRUIT CUP

*M*arsee likes to keep her meal preparation simple but nutritious. This colorful fruit cup, served as her first course, follows the rules of presentation over preparation. It takes only a few minutes to prepare each cup.

Marsee buys whatever seasonal fresh fruit is available, looking for choices that will add lots of color to the cup. This offering is infused with the bold colors of pomegranate seeds, Bing cherries, and blood oranges.

To add a bit of sparkle to this flavorful dish, Marsee dips the rims of her vintage martini stemware in lemon juice, then inverts the glasses in a plate of red sugar crystals to make each appear as if it were dusted with glitter. Red sugar is available at gourmet grocers and many grocery stores. It sparkles in the candlelight against the table's backdrop of red and silver.

To accompany the hearty beef tenderloin and potatoes, Marsee offers a colorful red and green vegetable medley that uses fresh cherry red tomatoes, green snap peas, and asparagus sautéed in olive oil and topped with Parmesan cheese. Marsee experiments with the seasonings, using red onion, lots of garlic, red pepper flakes, and black pepper.

She treats herself to a gourmet chocolate cake from her local gourmet grocer, so that she can sit down with her guests, assured that all of her time is not spent in the kitchen.

Christmas Morning

TWO WAYS

❦

After weeks of anticipation, Christmas Day arrives at last! This is a morning we wish would last forever. Cradling a cup of coffee, we wrap up in our robes and slippers and savor the sweetness of family.

For years, Marsee was treated to delightful Christmas mornings by her parents. So this year, she wants to spoil them for a change. First, she plays the carol "Joy to the World" on the stereo (the same music her parents used to wake up the children on Christmas morning). Then, as quiet as a mouse, she sneaks into the guest room where her parents sleep and leaves behind a breakfast tray filled with goodies to help start the morning off right.

Atop an antique desk, the silver tea service sparkles with the Christmas morning sun. Biscotti dipped in white chocolate, peppermint sticks capped with chocolate, and fragrant loose tea and a strainer promise a sweet beginning to the wonderful day.

After her parents enjoy a luxurious bath and a cup of tea in their room, they join the other guests for a light Christmas breakfast served informally in the kitchen. Marsee thinks Christmas morning should be spent basking in the glow of family—not cooking—so she keeps her breakfast fare simple.

Even the breakfast beverages are given a festive air on this merry day. The orange juice looks divine served in goblets accented with a skewer of fresh fruit. Instead of a standard tray, Marsee uses a mirror to hold the juice. But she doesn't stop there. She dusts the mirror with large sugar crystals that look like snow flakes, then threads a black ribbon proclaiming "Noel" through the stems of the glassware.

A day earlier, Marsee picked up a mouthwatering assortment of artichoke and spinach soufflés, cherry turnovers sprinkled with almonds, and blueberry Danish. To add visual interest to the serving tray, she creates ascending levels with cake plates, loading each with a bevy of fresh fruit. At the center of the tantalizing display is Marsee's son's family tree—a wire tree covered with tiny framed snapshots of family members.

A T THE GARRITY HOME,
I LIKE TO KEEP THINGS SIMPLE
ON CHRISTMAS MORNING, TOO,
SERVING A LIGHT BREAKFAST
IN OUR KITCHEN. I HAD FUN
DECKING THE ROOM IN A
PLAYFUL BLACK-AND-WHITE
THEME, ADDING ENOUGH
GREENERY TO MAKE THE NOOK

FEEL LIKE A WINTER FOREST.

EACH CHAIR SPORTS A SWAG

HELD IN PLACE BY A LARGE,

FESTIVE BOW. THE BLACK

TRANSFERWARE PLATES THAT

I USED ON MY PORCH TABLE

AT HALLOWEEN LOOK

COMPLETELY DIFFERENT

FRAMED WITH A WREATH AND

HUNG IN THE WINDOW.

Christmas Day

A GRAND TABLE AT THE GARRITY HOUSE

❦

Every year, Dan insists on hosting a magnificent Christmas dinner at our house, inviting family and close friends. We always look forward to the event with great anticipation, until we have to actually get dinner on the table while it's still hot. As we scramble, we begin to squabble. Our kitchen tiffs have become as much a family tradition as pumpkin pie, but as soon as we're all seated together, laughing and talking, our frustration evaporates into pure joy.

Instead of preparing each plate in the kitchen or squeezing large serving dishes onto my already-crowded table, I set up a dinner buffet on a round table in the center of my living room. The silver servers look magnificent under the boughs of a brilliantly lit Christmas tree, which makes a massive and impressive centerpiece.

At Christmas, my mother focused her energy on preparing a tantalizing meal. I put the same amount of attention into my holiday decor. And since all

good things at the Garrity house revolve around food, while Dan is preparing our traditional holiday dinner of beef tenderloin, I pour my heart into making my Christmas table a thing of beauty.

On my Christmas table this year, I pull the garden inside, setting up a provocative combination of opulent and rustic pieces. At each place I create a fragile tower of gold-rimmed china plates, then top them with a gritty stone pedestal and bird's nest.

When the evening is over, and we've waved good-bye to the last guests, I give myself a long-awaited Christmas gift, one I've earned during this hectic and wonderful season. I steal away and take a long winter nap.

*E*ACH YEAR, I SELECT A DIFFERENT THEME FOR MY DINING ROOM DECORATIONS, THEN BRING THE THEME TO LIFE LAYER BY LAYER, UNTIL THE TABLE IS FULL OF INTRIGUE AND WHIMSY. (MY GOAL IS TO SO CAPTIVATE GUESTS, THEY WON'T NOTICE IF THE MASHED POTATOES OR TURKEY HAVE GOTTEN A LITTLE COLD.)

MY ADVICE IS TO DO EVERYTHING YOU CAN AHEAD OF TIME SO YOU WON'T FEEL STRESSED AND FRENZIED ON CHRISTMAS DAY. ONE WAY TO GET A JUMP ON THE DAY IS TO DECORATE YOUR DINING ROOM IN ADVANCE. YOU'LL SEE THAT I CHANGED OUT MY FALL CHAIR COVERS WITH A BROWN AND CREAM LINEN PRINT.

THROUGHOUT THE ROOM, I PAIR DELICATE ITEMS FROM THE CHINA HUTCH AND ROUGH PIECES SNATCHED FROM THE SNOW-COVERED GARDEN. NEXT TO FORMAL SILVER CANDELABRA WITH TOWERING TAPERS, I DISPLAY AN AGED GARDEN URN, ROSES IN A WEATHERED TERRA-COTTA POT, AND PINECONES FROM MY YARD.

IN ADDITION TO COVERING THE CHANDELIER WITH GREENS, I HANG A SCRAGGLY PINE BOUGH FROM THE DINING ROOM CEILING. FROM ITS BRANCHES, I CASCADE BAUBLES LIKE BUD VASES, PRISMS, AND ORNAMENTS. UNDER THE BRANCH'S CANOPY, MY ELABORATELY DRESSED CHRISTMAS TREE SPORTS BOLD ORNAMENTS MIXED WITH TINY WHITE LIGHTS.

New Year's Eve

A SOPHISTICATED GATHERING
WITH A SIMPLE PLAN

❧

For some, the only way to properly bring in the New Year is to attend a formal gala, complete with ballroom dancing and a balloon drop. Others like to hop from party to party, while still others prefer a romantic evening alone with their significant other.

While I enjoy all manner of New Year's Eve celebrations, from the raucous to the refined, my favorite way to see out the old year and usher in the new is at a dinner party of good friends. After all the events of the Christmas season, by New Year's Eve, I'm usually ready to slow down a bit and spend time with special buddies, catching up, sharing stories, and laughing until our sides hurt.

So does my friend Marsee. Instead of going out on New Year's Eve, she plans an extraordinary event in her home. Marsee has a knack for making everything magical. One of her tricks is to set the scene before her guests arrive. Before you even walk through her door, she's lit every candle, cued the background music, and poured your favorite drink.

Build the Drama in Layers

Each place setting is composed of luscious layers, following the Nell Hill's way. Gold-rimmed dinner plates rest on gold chargers. Next comes a set of black-and-white transferware detailed with images of bees and birds. Two-handled china soup cups, ready to serve a cream-based gumbo, top the tower. A perfect New Year's Eve metaphor, contemporary champagne flutes stand alongside antique gilt-trimmed water glasses.

After you're silenced by the splendor of the table, you let out a shriek of delight when you notice the playful details added, like the lampshade-and-tiara-topped couple sauntering down the table's center. Alongside the dancing duo, an antique stopwatch counts down the minutes to midnight. A crafty friend fashioned the unique noisemakers from old sheet music and a German print of an 1889 New Year's Eve engraving. The ends are festooned with a fringe of black-and-silver paper.

Following her credo of "presentation over preparation," Marsee makes much of the meal ahead and buys many of the items ready made, including this grilled salmon entrée. That way she can spend time with guests, not slaving over a stove. Following a cup of hearty cream gumbo, guests indulge in a simple grilled salmon salad that is topped with potato shoestrings and accompanied by soft dinner rolls.

After guests have eaten their fill, they relax with drinks until a few minutes before midnight, when everyone gathers on the deck to light off fireworks and sparklers. This British dessert of layered fruit, pudding, and whipped cream is set ablaze as part of the midnight celebration. The fortune cookie predicts the new year will be full of the magic and joy that comes with surrounding yourself with wonderful friends.

Valentine's Day:

TABLE FOR TWO BY FIRELIGHT

❧

On this special day, surprise the special someone you love with a romantic dinner for two. I'm not one for spending Valentine's Day at an overcrowded and overpriced restaurant, opting instead to put on the ritz at home. I like to turn my living room into an intimate salon where Dan and I can indulge in a delicious dinner.

After seventeen years of marriage, one of my goals this year is to spoil my husband rotten. In the daily hustle and bustle, we don't always take the time we should to truly honor the most important people in our lives. That's why on Cupid's big day, I want to come up with inventive ways to let Dan know how much he means to me.

Instead of eating dinner in your dining room, on Valentine's Day try something different. Nestle a small side

table and two upholstered chairs up to the fireplace (it will be cozy enough there for you to wear that little black dress he loves). Or, pick another romantic nook in your home, like a bay window or alcove.

Then, cover your table in creamy white linens with red trim, and a full place setting of bone china tipped in red. Pull out the silver and crystal you just stowed away after the holidays, give it a shine, and use it liberally to add high style to your table. Not enough room to hold all your dinnerware and serving pieces? Use a small bench or side table as a buffet.

On Valentine's Day, you absolutely must have candlelight on your table. Remember, everyone looks beautiful basked in its warm glow. Even though it sounds clichéd, you've just got to have a bouquet of roses. If you have a yen for something unique, blend in other accessories that add to the romance of the evening. Use a beautiful book of love poems to bolster your silver teapot or play "your" song on the stereo.

For your dinner fare, select a dish he loves, yet is oh-so-easy to prepare, like chicken breast sautéed in olive oil, served on a bed of angel hair pasta.

⌀⌀

For fun, expand your menu to include side dishes that bring a touch of romance to the table. I couldn't resist the cheese and heart-shaped crackers I happened upon at a gourmet shop. Tantalizing dessert treats rest nearby for after-dinner nibbling.

Resources

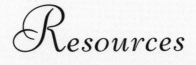

$\mathcal{M}$ost of the tabletop accessories in this book, unless otherwise noted, came from one of Mary Carol Garrity's three home furnishings stores. For complete information on her stores, visit www.nellhills.com. Mary Carol's stores are all located in Atchison, Kansas, at the following locations:

NELL HILL'S
501 Commercial Street
Atchison, KS 66002
(913) 367-1086
Gifts, accessories, and tabletop

G. DIEBOLTS
608 Commercial Street
Atchison, KS 66002
(913) 367-2395
Fabrics, bedroom, and bath

GARRITY'S ENCORE
121 N. 5th Street
Atchison, KS 66002
(913) 367-1523
Furniture and antiques

Many of the homeowners used their own dishes and accessories on the tables featured. This is a guiding principle of the Nell Hill's style of entertaining—always mix your own cherished pieces and family heirlooms with new items. In the text, we have pointed out where family heirlooms are featured, along with the homeowner's own dishes.

We would like to acknowledge all of the friends and business owners who helped us out in other cities, with sincere thanks and appreciation to the following businesses and individuals who helped in so many ways to make this book successful.

Floral arrangements:
Dianne Howard
Wichita, KS
(316) 260-8777

Flowers, gifts, and interiors:
Dean's Designs
Wichita, KS
(316) 686-6674

FAT TUESDAY
Beads, masks, feathers, and coins:
Oriental Trading Company
9101 F Street
Omaha, NE 68127
(800) 875-8480

Crab cakes:
Boudreau's Louisiana Seafood and Steaks
St. Joseph, MO
(816) 387-9911

LADIES' LUNCHEON
Seed packet designs:
Dianne Howard
Florist
Wichita, KS
(316) 260-8777

EASTER BRUNCH
Coconut/raspberry Easter cake:
Bert's Cookies
Kansas City, MO
(816) 931-4596

Elizabeth's Garden
Atchison, KS
(913) 367-1600

PICNIC IN THE PARK
Lemon meringue pie:
Jerry's Again Restaurant
Atchison, KS
(913) 367-0577

Chicken salad sandwiches:
Marigold's Bakery
Atchison, KS
(913) 367-3858

Paper placemat runner and sandwich paper:
Paper Source
Country Club Plaza
Kansas City, MO
(816) 753-2777

ENCHANTED SUMMER EVENING
Specialty cheese and Italian sausages:
The Better Cheddar
Prairie Village Shopping Center
Prairie Village, KS
(913) 362-7575

Needham Florists, Inc.
Kansas City, MO
(816) 523-5517

SIP AND SEE
Cupcakes:
Bert's Cookies
Kansas City, MO
(816) 931-4596

Packages and presents:
Greg Johnson Designs
(816) 931-4596

Village Flowers
St. Joseph, MO
(816) 232-3326

FALL MINI-FETE
Potato soup:
Cheryll Hartell
The Vineyard's Fine Dining
Weston, MO
(816) 640-5588

HALLOWEEN
Iced cookies:
Bert's Cookies
Kansas City, MO
(816) 931-4596

CHOCOLATE GATHERING
Gift boxes, bows, and ribbons:
Bradley Paper
Wichita, KS
(316) 684-3433

Chocolate candies:
Cero's Candy
Wichita, KS
(316) 264-5002

*Chocolate cake and gourmet
chocolates:*
Dean & Deluca
www.deandeluca.com

*Chocolate mice and chocolate-dipped
strawberries:*
Picadilly Market & Grill
Wichita, KS
 (316) 681-1100

Cinnamon sticks and specialty teas:
The Spice Merchant
Wichita, KS
(316) 263-4121

*Chocolate champignons, peppermint
sticks, cinnamon sticks, and decorative sugar:*
Williams-Sonoma
www.williams-sonoma.com

NEW YEAR'S EVE
Gold compote on table:
Juliana-Daniels Antiques
Wichita, KS
(316) 691-9966

Place cards and menu designs:
Marsee B's
Wichita, KS
(316) 630-9960

*New Year's Eve party horns
and tiara:*
Starla Morgan
Graphic Design
(316) 807-2985
fancifulsascinations@yahoo.com

VALENTINE'S DAY
Pillows and napkins:
Kathy Fernholz, Seamstress
Overland Park, KS
(913) 681-9524

Acknowledgments

❈

To Jean Lowe, my agent and good friend: Thank you for making this book and so many other wonderful things possible.

A special thank-you to Kerri Wagner, my extra set of eyes and hands for this book, who makes countless contributions to the "Nell Hill's style." I am especially grateful to Bryan McCay, who brings a creative spirit to everything and an incredibly calm approach to our work together. Micki Chestnut is so talented at crafting words and is able to channel my energy into pages of copy. I marvel at all of you!

I appreciate the contributions of the homeowners who made this book possible, not only for their generosity in opening up their homes and kitchens to us, but also their willingness to do anything to make this book a success: Marsee and Mike Bates, Brenda and Reed Graves, Ann and Guy Humphreys, and Barb and Bill Fricke. Thanks, too, for the excellent assistance from Gloria Case and Lynda Coulter, who are not only garden designers, but so talented at everything they do, as is Dianne Howard

with her floral arrangements and styling assistance, and Valerie Bean, who was willing to put in long, hard hours helping the crew in Wichita get the shots pulled together. I am so grateful to all of you.

A special thanks to my publisher, Andrews McMeel. Hugh Andrews has supported my publishing program from the start. Thanks to my editor, Dorothy O'Brien, for everything she did behind the scenes to make this book possible. We couldn't have done it without her and the great staff of Julie Barnes, Michelle Daniel, Diane Marsh, Caty Neis, and Julie Roberts. Thanks also to Jennifer Collet, Judi Marshall, and Rebecca Schuler for marketing the book, and to Cliff Koehler for producing it. Special thanks to Kathy Viele for her special sales efforts.

None of this would be possible without my dedicated, faithful store employees whose contributions to Nell Hill's success are immeasurable. I am so grateful to them for their help and talent. They are Melinda Allaman, Kathleen Armstrong, Glenna Batchelder, Jenny Bell, Audra Berry, George

Bilimek, Heather Brown, Carolyn Campbell, Ethel Campbell, Heather Clark, Shirley Cline, Suzanne Clizer, Joyce Colman, Abigail Compton, Debbie Cooney, Joe Domann, Jeff Federinko, Mary Kate Funk, Judy Green, Amy Hale, Carol Halem, Robert Hancock Jr., Brittaney Handke, Gail Hansen, Vicki Hinde, Kim Hobbs, Tamara Hurter, Dillon Kinsman, Sabrina Klutzke, Joy Kromer, Mary Kuckelman, Pat Kuckelman, Jennifer Latendresse, Nicky Liggett, June Lynn, Lesley Marlatt, Elsa Meyer, Amy Minnis, Shannon Mize, Danielle Moccia, Michelle Moccia, Nick Moore, Kathy Munson, Gloria Nash, Lois Niemann, Andrew Nolting, Simon Nolting, Cheryl Owens, Heather Owens, Susan Payne, Andrew Ramirez, Lanie Schaeffer, Mary Scheider, Roxann Schied, Alice Scott, Jamie Servaes, Kathy Sledd, Angie Stuebs, Gretchen Sullivan, Sarah Tucker, Tona Vanschoiack, Virginia Voelker, Jan Wessel, Lana White, Macy White, Margie Wilburn, Cyreesa Windsor, and Kay Wolfe.

Special thanks are also in order to JoAnne Baker, Chubby Darrenkamp, Jo Hines, Arty Long, Lara Nomokomov, Cecelia Pellettiere, Geraldine Weishaar, Marcelline Weishaar, Bill Wilson, and Norma Wilson.

I am blessed with dear friends who are always there for me. Many of them are acknowledged above, but the following people know how much I count on them:

Merrilee Bozzoli, Joan Carpenter, Melinda DiCarlo, Deann Dunn, Cheryl Hartell, Melanie Krumbholz, Darcy Mendenhall, and Nancy Neary.

And, always, my dear customers who keep coming back—I love you all!

Mary Carol Garrity